KECHARA

A Tsem Tulku Buddhist Organisation

Media & Publications

to Emmy

From Monlam

05 10 2010

If Not Now, When?

the **PEACE** edition

TSEM TULKU RINPOCHE

Compiled and Edited by
Sharon Saw and Jamie Khoo

Kechara Media & Publications
2009

Published by Kechara Media & Publications Sdn. Bhd.
5-2, Jalan PJU 1/3G
SunwayMas Commercial Centre
47301 Petaling Jaya
Selangor, Malaysia

Tel: (+603) 7805 5691   Fax: (+603) 7805 5690
Email: kmp@kechara.com
Website: kechara.com/kmp

The moral right of the author has been asserted.

ISBN 978 967 5365 18 8

First published by Kechara Media & Publications in 2008

Design by Fang Chyi Chang

Printed by Vivar Printing Sdn. Bhd.
Malaysia

CONTENTS

Tsem Tulku Rinpoche:
A Short Biography

Foreword

Editors' Preface

PROLOGUE

CHAPTER 01
013
DHARMA

CHAPTER 02
029
JOY
+sadness

CHAPTER 03
045
PEACE
+anger

CHAPTER 04
063
HARMONY
+conflict

CHAPTER 05
081
COMMITMENT
+ irresponsibility

CHAPTER 06
099
LOVE
+fear

CHAPTER 07
115
LIFE
+death

EPILOGUE

Tsem Tulku Rinpoche: A SHORT BIOGRAPHY

Beloved for his unconventional, contemporary approach to Dharma, H.E. Tsem Tulku Rinpoche brings more than 2,500 years of Buddhist wisdom and teachings to the modern spiritual seeker by connecting ancient worlds with new people, cultures, attitudes and lifestyles.

A Mongolian-Tibetan heritage, a childhood in Taiwan and in the United States of America, intensive monastic studies in India and now the Spiritual Guide of Kechara in Malaysia – these are but some of the many facets that contribute to Tsem Rinpoche's unique ability to effortlessly bridge the East and the West. His teachings bring the Dharma to our everyday lives and in doing so, he is able to bring the ancient, time-honoured Buddhist philosophies and practices into the 21st century.

Tsem Rinpoche has been strongly inclined towards Dharma since his early childhood and has studied under many great Buddhist masters of the Tibetan tradition. Tsem Rinpoche eventually went on to receive his monastic education at Gaden Shartse Monastery, currently located in south India.

Following the advice of his beloved Guru, H.H. Kyabje Zong Rinpoche, Tsem Rinpoche took his vows as a monk from H.H. the 14th Dalai Lama and joined Gaden Shartse Monastery in India when he was in his early twenties.

His two preceding incarnations, Gendun Nyedrak and Khentrul Rinpoche Thubten Lamsang, had also studied at Gaden Shartse Monastery when it was then located in Tibet. There, they obtained Geshe Lharam degrees before completing their studies at Gyuto tantric college.

Gendun Nyedrak went on to become the lead chanter and, later, abbot of Gaden Monastery, while Khentrul Rinpoche brought the Dharma to the laypeople of the Phari district of Tibet. The tremendous and virtuous work of his previous lifetimes can perhaps be seen again in Tsem Rinpoche's present-day activities, where he continues this selfless practice of teaching vast numbers of non-monastic communities in places where the Dharma has just begun to bloom.

During his nine years in Gaden, Tsem Rinpoche was involved in extensive charitable works including building schools for refugee children in India, building dormitories and upgrading living conditions for the monastic community, and providing long-term assistance to the poor lay community of Mundgod.

Now, based in Malaysia and Nepal, Tsem Rinpoche continues this immense work to benefit many. Through creative and engaging approaches, Tsem Rinpoche continuously shares new methods of bringing happiness and relief to people from all walks of life. Tsem Rinpoche also maintains close contact with Gaden Monastery, and through his constant practice of generosity and deeply altruistic motivation, continues to frequently sponsor Gaden's work and activities.

Be inspired by H.E. Tsem Tulku Rinpoche's work and life at www.tsemtulku.com

His Eminence Kensur Dakpa Tenzin Rinpoche ABBOT EMERITUS OF GADEN SHARTSE MONASTERY

Of the six *paramitas*[1] , generosity is listed as the first and the one from which the other five arise. Teaching the Dharma is considered the most supreme form of giving for it is through learning and practising the Dharma methods that we gain the wisdom to relieve ourselves of suffering.

These days, however, people are generally less inclined towards seeking and studying a spiritual path. The illusive search for money, fame and an often false sense of security and happiness takes away our time from discovering what it really means to tap into the endless joy within ourselves. So how, indeed, are we to learn a new way, other than the one we're so comfortable – yet unhappy – with?

2,500 years ago, the Buddha laid down a set of teachings that would encompass 84,000 methods, to suit the dispositions of just as many types of minds. In anticipating the decline of spiritual practice in our times, Buddha showed us ways to engage in a higher path in spite of our many distractions. Then, to make these teachings accessible and joyously relevant to the 21st Century world, there are the teachers of today. Vibrant, dynamic, young Lamas like Tsem Tulku Rinpoche understand the superficial, disconnected worlds

[1] Enlightened qualities that help us to progress in our spiritual practice and eventually attain liberation from suffering: Generosity, Patience, Joyous Effort, Ethics, Meditative Concentration and Wisdom.

that we live in now and are able to show us a bridge that can link us back to ourselves.

Tsem Tulku Rinpoche's vast yet intimate personal experiences within both Western and Eastern cultures as well as his thorough understanding and attainments of Dharma wisdom – through many lifetimes of ardent study and practice – brings all his teachings to life. They are relevant, easy to understand and resonate because they are drawn from his own realisation and practice of these teachings. Tsem Rinpoche embodies everything he teaches and works tirelessly to bring this clarity to all his students too.

The teachings in this book may seem simple and short, but it is through this simplicity that we understand the real depth of what it means to follow a spiritual path. It is exactly because the teachings seem so simple that we are pushed harder to bring them fully into our daily lives and activity. Realising and attaining them is rewarding and infinitely beneficial to us and those around us for they carry a profound and lasting impact that can change people's entire lives.

Tsem Tulku Rinpoche gives his students and readers the biggest gift he could in offering these teachings to the world. Now, you hold the gift in your hands. By taking this advice to heart and using each one to discover the luminous nature within, you give yourself the highest gift of all. I pray always that the wisdom within these pages may inspire you thus.

EDITORS' PREFACE

This book was borne out of our wish to share personal text messages that H.E. Tsem Tulku Rinpoche often sent to his students. When we started work on the book in 2007, other quotations from His Eminence's teachings were added to complement the existing selection of quotations. The final volume comprised a spectrum of quotations from various teachings which addressed universal issues of Joy and Sadness, Harmony and Conflict, Commitment and Irresponsibility, Love and Fear, and Life and Death.

When *If Now Now, When?* was finally published a year later in 2008, the book met with an enthusiastic, resonating response from readers who often approached us directly to tell us how much the teachings had helped to lift their spirits and inspire their lives. It was exciting and wonderful to see how short paragraphs and single lines were making a difference, and to hear that they were being readily and joyfully integrated into the daily lives of many.

Now, we revisit the book in this PEACE edition which features a new chapter, "Peace and Anger". In this and all other chapters, we have added new and previously unpublished quotations from His Eminence which speak specifically on the theme of cultivating inner and outer peace. Ultimately, every chapter in the book shows us a new way for achieving this peace – we just have to find it within us and make it shine.

As editors of the book, we had the rather impossible job of selecting the quotations from an incredible wealth of teachings. Every single one struck a chord and brought to light a different teaching. The final collection of quotations you now hold in your hands was chosen for their beautifully simple, honest and uplifting insights which continue to resonate in our hearts, no matter how many times we have read them. We hope you will enjoy this book as much as we have enjoyed compiling it and that the wisdom within touches your hearts as much as they have ours.

Sharon Saw & Jamie Khoo

PROLOGUE

Verses that move our minds,
Words that compel us to think,
Thoughts that shame us to change,
Ideas that crystallise our feelings,
Remain ink and paper if unapplied.

Stories of past marvels and great beings,
Miracles, adventures, journeys and hardships
That serve to inspire and transform,
Bringing tears, emotions and courage,
Remain ink and paper if unapplied.

Buddhas, Bodhisattvas, Arhats, Saints,
Their words, teachings, ideas and attainments,
Are worth only the ink and paper they are
printed on if unapplied.

I hope these pages will be worth more than just ink and paper.

CHAPTER 01

DHARMA

Dharma is not about who is right and who is wrong; it is not about whose centre is big; it is not about which religion is right; it is not about whether there is a next life or not; it is not about whether Buddha exists or God exists; it is not about whether Catholicism is the real religion or Buddhism is the real religion: it is not about any of that. It is about us bringing harmony into our families, into our lives and to the people we care about NOW. That is what it is about. And that is what we learn Dharma for.

The greatest mind is not about wanting other people to change;
but you yourself changing and accepting other people.

The greatest mind is to stop thinking when **THEY** will change.
No. We should think, "**When will I change?**"

photograph by VENKAT SRINIVASAN

The effect we have on others when we make them happy
without motive and when their mind is happy because of us –
that is Dharma.

If you have one less argument with your partner, **that is Dharma**.
If you have one less attachment, **that is Dharma**.
If you control your anger once a day, **that is Dharma**.
If you forgive your partner, **that is Dharma**.

That is what Dharma is: bringing people together.

You want to be spiritual?

Buy flowers for your wife. Stop nagging your husband.

Take your wives out to eat. Don't cheat on your husbands and wives, in any way.

You want the greatest practice?

The greatest practice is getting behind a steering wheel and taking your mother and father out to eat.

You want the greatest mantra?

The greatest mantra is, "How are you, Mummy? How are you, Daddy? What can I do for you?"

That is the greatest mantra at this moment, for us.

You don't give up your job because you're not rich.

You keep working until you're rich (whatever your definition of rich is).

It would be stupid to say, "I'm not rich, I give up".

So how can you say, "Certain people don't practise the Eight Verses of Transforming the Mind

and therefore, I'm not going to do it"?

That's all the more reason you should do it.

That's all the more reason you should be involved.

That's all the more reason you should practise.

THE
GLORIOUS
DEAD

1914 - 1918
1939 - 1945

浩氣長存　英魂不朽

You're not practising on the basis of you getting something. You're practising on the basis that something is lacking so you wish to give. We do not do Dharma practice based on other people, situations or environments. We do Dharma practice for other people, for other situations and for other environments.

Dharma allows you to keep and have what you have but the motive and purpose of having it changes so the results also change. For example, now we might think, "I will eat so I can be the strongest and surpass everyone else." After knowing Dharma, we think, "I will eat so my body has strength to benefit others." The act of eating remains the same but the motive and purpose become different. Therefore, the act of eating itself creates **positive karma** due to the change of our motive.

If we apply the same thing to all our activities, then engaging in them would not bring negative results. That is how we can remain the "same" on the outside but have huge transformation on the inside.

When someone shouts at you, when someone scolds you, when someone is rude to you, when someone has abused you or is hurting you, when someone doesn't agree with you or opposes you – that is when you practise the Dharma.

photograph by KECHARA

photograph by **WEI YEIN LEONG**

Spiritual practice is not about going to places and chanting, knowing the stuff and debating. Spiritual practice is the transformation of our perspective and how we look at things. It is how much our mind has changed from negative to positive. That is spiritual practice.

holiness

Holiness is not a state of you having a halo.
Holiness is you trying harder.

photograph by TEE BOON PEEN

Universally, whatever country, race or religion, the thought of taking pain and suffering for others onto ourselves, quietly and secretly, is true spirituality.

Surrender means opening up your wounds, pain, suffering and desires. **Surrender** means you are ready to hear the truth.

Whether we believe in a next life or in heaven is not as important as how we treat others now.

Imagine one day of not lying, not having negative motivations or attachments.
Imagine one day of thinking only of others, non-stop. That whole day is filled
with light, love, compassion, clairvoyance, skill and great planning for others
– **an altruistic mind.**

CHAPTER 02
JOY
+sadness

If you believe in God, that's fabulous;
if you believe in Buddha, that's fabulous;
if you don't believe in anything, that's fabulous.
But please believe in yourself and please
believe in the happiness you can bring to the
people around you. Believe in that.
Wouldn't that be lovely?

We can bring joy to others if we have controlled our minds. We can control our minds if we take any holy being's teachings – of

BUDDHA

MOHAMMED

JESUS CHRIST

KRISHNA

– and we really sincerely practise them, not just follow blindly, then we will see a big difference.

photograph by TEE BOON PEEN

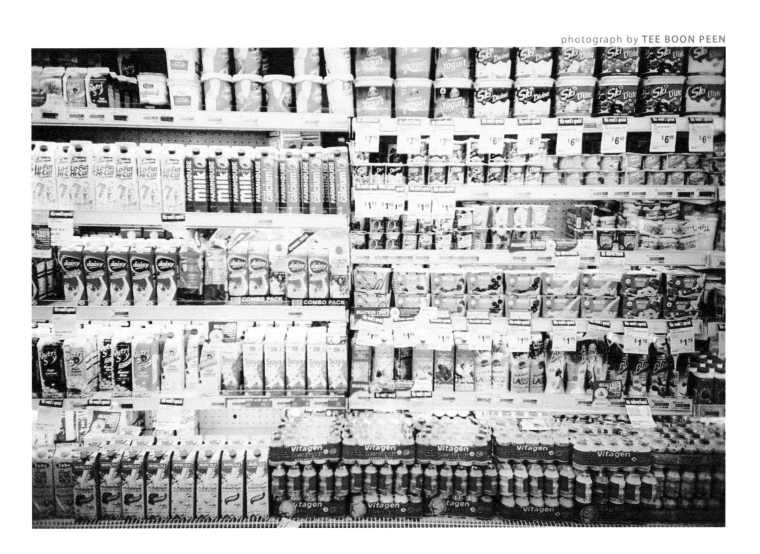

What is right or wrong is how happy or unhappy you feel. And feeling happy or unhappy is not determined solely by an outer, physical environment. It is a state of mind.

The secret is not to give up money, position, your wife, your husband or your children – the secret here is to do what you need to do for them but to realise you are only here for a short time. If you keep existing only for making yourself happy based on external objects, you will not be happy because those are not the causes of happiness. If you have experienced any "happiness" from these external objects, it is false, it is made up, it is you telling yourself you are happy. Actually, you are not.

The ones with the biggest position, the biggest name and the biggest wealth will suffer the most because everything reinforces their fears and their non-perception of reality.

photograph by KECHARA

Stop looking for reasons not to practise.

Stop looking for reasons to be unhappy.

Where has that gotten you?

Surrender! If you do not want to be happy for yourself, then be happy for the people you claim you love. Make them happy by being happy yourself.

Because I'm depressed, I don't have to do anything, improve, change, be responsible and just remain stagnant year after year... I wonder if it's the very deep self-centred mind under the cloak of depression that fools myself and which I hide behind??

photograph by MUN LEE

I, I, I,
Me, Me, Me,
Me,
Myself, Myself,
Myself,
Myself,

CHERISH ME REGARDLESS...

with this "mantra" at our core,
why ask "why" when things are unfulfilled?

Things I "like" Manjushri Buddha, Coke, gifts, Dharma books, my Gurus, being thin, Gaden, mountains, *Mahasiddhas*, Tantra, great statues, DVDs, Yogi my dog, *Bodhicitta*, self-worth, giving gifts, health, Malaysia, Madonna, Star Trek, Wonder Woman, Bodhgaya, Japan, pizza and being sponsored…

Things I "dislike" club soda, cellulite, tourist *thangkas*, stinginess, three lower realms, death, poverty, beaches, steamed vegetables, gym, exercises, travelling, Ford pick-up trucks, ego, flu, aging, weirdoes, cruelty, rain, sushi, narrow minds, animal abuse, small beds, Willie Nelson, dirty and uncontrolled rebirth.

" I don't know where my likes and dislikes actually really lead me to but one thing is certain: In order to truly be surrounded by what I like and avoid what I don't like, I always need to not have likes and dislikes, and just accept… "

We endure pain with suffering because we are attached to ego – we do not want to have suffering, we are selfish, we do not care if other people experience suffering.

However, if we endure pain without attachment, we will be able endure it; we will not suffer. In fact, the very pain we have will increase our happiness because we are accepting the pain, problems and difficulties for the sake of others.

photograph by **TEE BOON PEEN**

The key to happiness is taking our strongest affliction, working on it and chipping away at it over time. When we chip away at it over time, we will see it lessen. When that lessens, the reactions that would have arisen from that mind will also lessen. When the reactions that arise from that mind lessen, the counter-reactions back to us from others will also lessen. Then, we will experience more peace.

A direct, long term and permanent SOLUTION for **depression** is the continuous practice of GIVING:

giving of time, love, help, advice, care, Guru devotion, giving to the Sangha, giving medicine, money, shelter, Dharma, practice, devotion and material needs to others continuously without self-centred motive,

especially to those who cannot benefit themselves. In time, **you will see depression lessen** and its **duration shorten** as a direct and immediate result of giving.

In giving to others, you give to yourself; in giving to yourself, you give to others because the happier you become, the more you can do for others. And the only way to create happiness for yourself is by making other people happy.

[There are people who have pursued helping others and they are much happier than people who pursue themselves.]

CHAPTER 03
PEACE
+anger

If we are going to pray for and benefit the world, we should start with the people we live with. We don't talk about world peace, we talk about the people we live with.

photograph by **VENKAT SRINIVASAN**

There is no **ONE** cause for world peace but if you had to pick,
then eradicate the self-centred mind first. The rest will follow.

Peace cannot be left as an unattainable goal. If we apply effort, it is achievable.

If

we

do

not

create

inner

peace

outer

peace

is

not

possible.

As a result of
the selfish mind,
we have global warming,
we have war and conflicts.
All this arises from
the selfish mind.

Speech
is
the
cause
of
war
as
well
as
peace.

photograph by **LINDA SEE**

Assumptions make war,
clarifications lead to peace.

Anger is impermanent; disharmony is impermanent. We must ask ourselves where we will be once that is over. That is more important than the moment of anger.

Deception, **stealing** and **lying** are causes for small-scale wars that lead to the loss of inner peace for others and ourselves.

photograph by **FANG C. CHANG**

Not getting revenge is a true sign of inner peace and strength.

CHOOSE TO BE PART OF THE PROBLEM OR PART OF THE SOLUTION.

Anger is quick and it passes
but its effects are worse than
EARTHQUAKES
and its after-effects stay.
Why create earthquakes
when there are none?

photograph by **KECHARA**

Controlling one's anger one step at a time leads to balance and peace.

photograph by WEI YEIN LEONG

Do not hold anger, it benefits no one.

Do not act out of anger, you will only be ashamed afterwards.

Do not incite anger because you will get burned.

Be the first to make peace.

Be the peacemaker and wherever you go, you will be loved and be able to love.

A tear can be ego and anger can be compassion.
Anger can be ego and tears can be compassion.
It depends on where it arises from.

CHAPTER 04

HARMONY
+conflict

It is easy to be nice to someone who is nice to you. They are nice to you, you are nice to them. That is not religion, that is not spiritualism, that is not Catholicism, that is not Jesus, that is not Buddha, that is not God. It is nice and easy to be nice to someone who is nice to you, but it is not easy to be nice to someone who is not nice to you. Religion and spiritual practice is being nice and patient to people who are not to you.

photograph by LINDA SEE

When a person whom you have benefited and in whom you have placed great hope hurts you, it is not that person who has hurt you. It is your wrong intent, wrong motive and wrong projection toward that person that have hurt you.

photograph by **VENKAT SRINIVASAN**

If people react negatively to you, and you react in the same way, then you are just the same as them. But, you say, they started it. Yes, they did but you continued it. What is the difference?

If we have been having arguments with our wife, we should stop thinking, "Why is my wife like that?" Maybe we should start thinking, "Why do I react to my wife like that?" and let go and change ourselves.

A PERSON'S OUTER ACTION REFLECTS HIS INNER MIND.

Envy and jealousy are very harmful because you are never ever satisfied with what you have and you never reflect on what you have. You constantly live your life based on what you do not have.

photograph by **U-EN NG**

photograph by **MICHAELANGELO MORAN**

Let others win whether they are right or wrong. Let go of conventions, rules, projections, expectations. JUST BE and do not let any experience which happens every moment be another factor for us to create more unhappiness because everything fades, just the results remain.

Because we share this small space together, time is short, we are overwhelmed with the results of our own past doings and we want to make Dharma goals a reality for many, we MUST LEARN TO get along by changing OUR minds. It is not a dream but has BECOME A NECESSITY!

Rejoice in the good actions that you have done and increase them. **Recognise the faults that you have and work on them.** And when you make a mistake, get up and try again. When we do that, respect for people, cultures and religions all arise from our minds as well as acceptance of people and of how they should be. And we come out of our box. **Wisdom arises.**

photograph by **LINDA SEE**

Ask yourself, at this point in your life, if you are still trying to win an argument and if that is the most important thing to you. If you are 40, 50, 60, 70 years old and you are still trying to win year after year, you have wasted your life. That may have been what you needed 30, 40, 50 years ago, but why are you still at that level? Why do you still need to win?

When corrected, watch that your

mind does not automatically cover

the fault. Examine the fault deeply

instead. Cultivate great appreciation

that someone pointed out the fault at

all. The pain you feel when someone

brings your faults out in the open is

small compared to the suffering you

cause others with your faults.

When we say **"I am sorry"** from the heart, it is not necessarily about whether we are wrong. By habituation, we might have done something to make someone unhappy. If we say sorry, it is because we are sorry that someone is unhappy.

photograph by **FANG C. CHANG**

A good person's quality is to step out first because he wants to make himself and everybody around him happy.

Being humble doesn't mean you lose; it means you have won.

Give the victory to others.

Stop sitting there bellyaching and complaining about what you do not have. You may never have it for the rest of your life so do you want to spend the rest of your life complaining about not having it? Or accept it and make others around you happy? Sometimes, living peacefully with our partners, friends and family is a gift in itself. Sometimes not shouting, screaming and fighting is a gift in itself, because where can we buy that?

We keep looking outside for the light when we should now become the light.

We want to be skinny but we don't control eating.

We want affection but we push away those who shower us with it.

We want to be free of debts but we recklessly spend.

We want love but we don't want to accommodate and change.

We want a good reputation but we don't act in ways that invite it.

We want people to help but do we really help?

We want respect but we run away when it gets tough.

We want blessings but without any commitments.

We want freedom from problems but we run from remedies.

We are frustrated and we don't know much but we don't want to study.

We want a good body but we don't want to exercise or diet.

CHAPTER 05

COMMITMENT
+irresponsibility

We want clairvoyance but we don't engage in retreats.

We want understanding but we create confusion with our non-commitment.

We want clarity of our intentions but without effort.

We want not to be misunderstood but our words are elusive.

We want blessings and affection but without devotion.

We want constant support but we don't make time for others.

We don't want conflict but we break our word of honour.

We want smiles, nice words and acceptance but we are hard and unforgiving.

We pray but our prayers don't bear fruit.

We hate problems but we ignore the real cause of it.

We are lonely and lost because renunciation is just a big word.

When we want to get something, acquire or accomplish anything with lasting results, there are many ways and levels to attract it. If it is by looks, then we need to be disciplined in diet and exercise, etc. If it is by knowledge, then we need to put effort into studying. If it is by wealth, we need to make a lot of personal sacrifice and work hard over a period of time. If it is by a kind heart and maturity, then we have to mentally train ourselves through awareness, practice and consistency. Whatever the method, effort with results is the key.

When we do things continuously and with effort, there will be results. When we do it sporadically, our results will be sporadic. If we only go to the gym once every six months, we will look like we only go to the gym once every six months. If we only drive by a gym once every six months, we will look like we only drive by a gym once every six months. Similarly, if we meditate, focus, practise and control our minds with the Dharma every single day, we will look like we control our minds. We will look like we are practising the Dharma. We will see transformation.

If you blame others for everything wrong in your life, you give control over your life to them. If you control your life, you cannot blame others.

(Saving does not come from an outer source.
It comes from yourself.)

Courage is not doing something in the absence of fear but knowing that something else is more important than fear. So we do it.

Not liking something indicates something deeper. Avoiding what we do not like does not help our mind overcome these self-imposed difficulties and improve to have peace.

SOLUTION Face it head on. When you come to a crossroad, always pick the more difficult path because when you apply yourself, you will see the difficulties become easier. Next time, what was difficult before will not be difficult anymore.

photograph by **KECHARA**

photograph by **MARCUS LIM**

The heroes we see in everyday life are just like you and me, except they are not afraid to be wrong, to admit their mistakes or to admit they are afraid. And in spite of the mistakes and fear, they achieve what they set out to do anyway.

photograph by **WEI YEIN LEONG**

It is only when you fall down that you can see how strong you are. When you fall down and you stay down – and you complain, bitch, make people feel sorry for you, want people to give you things – it shows you your lack of strength. It is when you fall down and you are humble, you push yourself and you can never stop that shows that you really practise.

photograph by **MARCUS LIM**

When you say you can do something, you may fail and fall flat on your face.
That does not mean you have not achieved it – it means you are on the road to achieving it.

photograph by **FANG C. CHANG**

Perhaps going after goals and commitments is another tactic to delay committing to compassion.

photograph by **VENKAT SRINIVASAN**

If we look around us, if we are very honest with ourselves and examine the difficulties we have in our lives, we should begin to question where these difficulties came from. **Who gave them to us? Who created them?** We have to be very honest, in the silence of our rooms, alone with our minds and we have to ask ourselves, "Was I the cause and author of all of this?" If we are honest with ourselves, we will realise that we most likely were.

photograph by LINDA SEE

Commitment is not about how many obstacles you face. **Commitment** is about how much you want it.

When someone tells you something you do not like, push yourself **to listen**. Push yourself **to be open**. Push yourself **to change** your habit of closing people out.

Gymnasts, lazy people, complainers and successful people have all practised to be what they are good at. So if you keep practising being lazy, you will be lazy. If you keep practising complaining, you will always complain. If you practise compassion, generosity, patience, working hard and having a bigger vision, you will become better at it with time because you will create the causes to become better. **YOU ARE PRACTISING TO BECOME BETTER.**

Why run away, avoid and deny? Why not give in to concern, acting for others, great love, generosity, offering of time, effort or care for others, acceptance, patience and calm abiding? That is who we really are… If Enlightenment is not within, then where might it be? ▪

CHAPTER 06

LOVE
+fear

Don't look for love. Create it with whoever you meet.

Don't look for respect. Be humble and sow the seeds to be respected and cherished.

Don't look for kind words. Speak to others kindly and you will get it naturally.

Don't have ill motive for money, gain and possessions from others

and you will gain others' trust, confidence and help.

Don't find and magnify your own endless problems but solve, listen to

and find solutions for others' turmoil.

Then you will grow within and without.

Loving others does not mean you neglect yourself. It just means you find better ways to love yourself through others.

photograph by **MICHAELANGELO MORAN**

We transform our minds because we love people – we love our parents, our spouses, our lovers, our friends and the people around us. We transform our minds out of love. It is not something negative that we have to do.

Serve your parents, drive them around, feed them, call them, take care of them, massage them, make time for them, listen to them, listen to them tell the same story 5,000 times, smiling and happily ask them what happened again and again and again. Do you know why? That is all that is left. And when I speak about parents, I mean anyone who has been kind to you.

photograph by **VENKAT SRINIVASAN**

Everything that we have is only for a very, very short time. And the most important thing in our lives are the people who care about us – these are the people who have loyally stayed with us and who have been by our side through our bad habits, bad temper, bad words and anger. It is these people – who have stayed with us over time – who are important. In the end, we might lose everything except these people.

photograph by **GARY YAP**

Everyone disappoints you. Do you know why everyone disappoints you? Because you are hanging on to a projection, you are hanging on to how they should be, you are hanging on to how you should be treated. You are not thinking about them, you are not thinking about others. You are thinking about yourself. That is why you become depressed.

photograph by **FANG C. CHANG**

Being lonely is something that everyone fears.

What they do not understand is that loneliness is a state of mind, it is not who you are with or not with. You could be with someone and be extremely lonely - you cannot relate to them or understand them. When some people are with other people, they are even lonelier than they were without anyone. Some people are alone but not lonely.

Loneliness is not about being with someone or having to be with someone. Loneliness is a state of mind where we do not accept who we are inside and what we need to improve. We therefore need to be distracted with other people to make us look away from ourselves.

Loneliness is not about being somewhere, being something, having something or being with someone. Loneliness is about not daring to look at our faults and pushing towards improvement, and therefore, wanting to be distracted from what we see in ourselves that we do not like. So, we surround ourselves with loud music, parties, beautiful people, friends, music, books... We want to have anything and everything to not think about what we are inside.

COMPASSION

Compassion is realising that others want the same thing as we do. But we also realise that they are more and each of us are only one, so working for the majority is correct.

photograph by **LINDA SEE**

A wish-granting jewel can confer on you material gains but a negative person or a person who hurts you can confer on you Enlightenment because they give you the greatest opportunity to practise patience, compassion and love. They are the greatest test to see if you have compassion and love.

The secret is to accept people as they are and not what you have mentally made them into – as monsters or as angels. All monsters are wrongly afflicted perceptions. And so are all angels.

photograph by **U-EN NG**

The people who complain, have difficulties, who are bitchy and problematic, the people who don't transform, and the people who create gossip and problems – **forgive them, love them, transform them by your example, and give them hope and courage by your persistence and effort of not giving up.** Do not criticise, gossip, talk about them, write about them or say things about them, but in response to their harm, give them benefit.

To hate and to have hate is not reality because it is based on afflicted emotion. Hatred or anger is not natural, it is not permanent, it is not your real state of mind. And afflicted emotions do not focus on reality or how the object is really existing; it is how we perceive them.

photograph by **KECHARA**

Compassion, this ability to love
others, regardless of what they do
to us, is our true nature.

GOD and BUDDHA

cannot get rid of hatred but

a development of love

within ourselves can.

Forgiveness is the start.

photograph by U-EN NG

You experience **compassion** when you give it, not when you get it.

CHAPTER 07

LIFE
+death

Time passes fast. Situations change. Whatever we work so hard to accomplish in life vanishes fast. People age fast. People die and they never come back as we know them, so we have to make the best of it while they are here with us now. Do not let simple obstacles – laziness, fear, avoidance, excuses – stop you from doing the best you can for people who have been kind to you in many ways.

Time and death of people will not stand still for you to finish your project, plans, works and wishes. If the real reason for what we are doing now is to bring happiness to those we care about, and we neglect, mistreat, forget them or make them sad, then how do we know they will still be around or alive when we are ready?

We talk about
death so
we can live.

We realise death
so we can make
others live.

photograph by **MUN LEE**

photograph by **LINDA SEE**

In life, everything passes by very quickly and whatever has happened in the past does not matter anymore – it becomes like a dream. In time, even the dream fades. But the results from that "dream" do not fade. Eventually, we will have to experience these results so we need to be aware of what we are doing right now that will be the cause for those results.

I AM RIGHT

i am wrong

your way

MY way

I can't I WON'T

I shan't

I **AM** that way...

I am, I am, I am...

With death so near, what does it matter??

photograph by **WEI YEIN LEONG**

Accept that things have to go, accept that things have to change,
accept that things have to degenerate, accept that all things do not belong to you eventually.

No matter how beautiful you are, you will not be beautiful one day; no matter how rich you are, your wealth will be taken away at the time of death.

If we were to die tonight, close our eyes, have an accident;
if our plane was to crash, if we ate something wrong, if
we choked, got robbed or shot – if any of these things
were to happen to us and if today was our last day to live,
then what would be the value of the things that we have
done from the time we were born until now?

Time is short.

Opportunities will be lost.

If you think you are young

and you are going to live forever,

the people around you

who you care about will not

be young and live forever.

Yes, your difficulties and your

problems are genuine,

they are real,

but they will also pass.

The conditions for someone to be perfect are impermanent. The conditions for someone to be imperfect are impermanent too — do not be attached to either.

photograph by **VENKAT SRINIVASAN**

I want you to have another perspective. Right now, tonight, you find out your husband or your wife died. They died. No more. You go home and your partner, your friend, your mother, your daughter, your sister, your wife, your husband is dead.

You go home alone.

Now, how do you feel? Now, who wins? What about the latest argument? The latest nagging session? The latest fight? The last time you sat there in anger and thought, "They did this and they did that to me"? And you know what is the fear behind all that? It will happen. None of us can escape that.

YES to friends, to lovers, to business meetings!

YES to dinners and parties!

YES to dates, drinks, entertainment, watching TV, eating and shopping! But when something is wrong, how, where and who? Friends and lovers leave. Parties always end. Shopping is only a temporary therapy and leads to debts.

Yes, we need business and money but how much is enough? What is the limit? Dinners are lovely but what do they lead to?

At the end of this, we sit back and, while flossing our teeth, we feel a deep sense of loneliness, senselessness and purposelessness. Not because we are bad, but because we have been focusing too much for too long on the wrong agendas to happiness. Perhaps our activities are not balanced. We need a consistent balance in life between the spiritual and the material.

photograph by **VENKAT SRINIVASAN**

photograph by MARCUS LIM

Ants work so hard to drag crumbs, dig and build anthills, jostle to mate with each other and then maybe "securely" die. In between, someone may step on their anthill, it might rain or myriads of other incidences might arise to take away their hard-earned security. Our life is like that but just longer. No matter where we are, there is no security in *samsara*.

As long as we continue to work towards that sense of security, we will become disillusioned, depressed and tumble down, no matter how "high" we get. No matter how much we build our lives towards this, it will be constantly threatened, taken away or we will lose it in the end. And because of our strong habituated belief that **THERE IS SECURITY,** our sufferings arise.

■ What matters is right now. How you react.

photograph by MARCUS LIM

EPILOGUE

I humbly request you all to continue your spiritual journey. It does not matter whether it is with us, on your own or somewhere else. But do continue with your spiritual journey.

photograph by KECHARA

APPENDIX THE EIGHT VERSES OF TRANSFORMING THE MIND

by Geshe Langri Tangpa

By realising that all sentient beings
Are more precious than wish-granting jewels,
For attainment of the supreme goal,
May I always hold them dear to my heart!

Whenever I associate with anyone,
May I view myself as least of all,
And, from the depths of my heart,
May I cherish others as supreme!

During all actions, as soon as thoughts
Or delusions arise in my mind
That are harmful to myself and others,
May I stop them with effective means!

As for sentient beings who are bad-natured,
When I see they are oppressed by negativity and pain,
May I cherish them just like I am encountering
A precious treasure that is difficult to find!

May I accept unjust loss
Such as others abusing me,
Or slandering me out of jealousy,
And may I offer the victory to others!

And if someone I have helped,
One for whom I had great hopes,
Harms me without slightest reason,
May I view him as my holy Guru!

In brief, directly and indirectly,
I offer aid and joy to all my mothers!
May I secretly take upon myself
All harm and suffering of my mothers!

May all of this be undefiled
By stains of the eight mundane views,*
And through discernment knowing all things as illusion,
Without grasping, may all be released from bondage!

* The eight mundane views, also known as the eight worldly concerns, are the desire to counter pleasure, material gain, praise and fine reputation; and the desire to avoid pain, material loss, blame and bad reputation.

GLOSSARY

Arhat – highly attained sages.

Bodhicitta – the determination to attain Enlightenment to liberate all living beings from suffering.

Buddha – the Awakened One. The term "Buddha" refers to all Beings that have attained full Enlightenment.

Dharma – right conduct: seeing, thinking, feeling, speaking and acting in ways conducive to lasting happiness, as propagated in the teachings of Buddha Shakyamuni. Dharma does not refer to just Buddhist teachings but also to teachings in all religions which give this same message of a right way of attaining happiness and helping others.

Eight Verses of Mind Transformation – an ancient mind transformation prayer. See Appendix.

Enlightenment – a state of mind purified of all delusions, with the positive qualities of wisdom, compassion and skilful means fully activated.

Guru – Sanskrit for "Teacher" or "Spiritual Guide".

Guru Devotion – Having great faith in, and commitment and loyalty to one's Guru. We submit ourselves fully to his teachings and carry out his instructions, with the understanding that this relationship will bring us all the way to Enlightenment.

Karma – literally, "action" in Sanskrit. Karma refers to the universal law of cause and effect. This suggests that all positive, negative and neutral actions of our body, speech and mind will have a corresponding reaction.

Mahasiddhas – supremely attained Beings.

(Six) Paramitas – also known as the Six Perfections. Enlightened qualities that help us to progress in our spiritual practice and eventually attain liberation from suffering: Generosity, Patience, Joyous Effort, Ethics, Meditative Concentration and Wisdom.

Samsara – the cycle of existence where sentient beings continue to create and experience their own sufferings lifetime after lifetime.

Sangha – the community of monks and nuns. On an absolute level, this refers to the field of all enlightened Beings.

Tantra – the practice of taking the result onto the path where we identify with and work directly with the energies and qualities of enlightened Beings.

Thangka – traditional Tibetan paintings, usually of deities.

Three Lower Realms – the animal, spirit and hell realms.

SOURCES CITED

The quotations within this book have been extracted from public teachings given by H.E. Tsem Tulku Rinpoche, as well as from personal messages that he has sent to his students.

These teachings are also available as books and DVDs, all of which are published and produced by Kechara Media & Publications.

BOOKS

- Compassion Conquers All: Teachings on the Eight Verses of Mind Transformation, 2007
- Gurus for Hire, Enlightenment for Sale: An Insider's Guide into the Relationship Between Spiritual Teachers, Students and Centres, 2009
- Nothing Changes, Everything Changes, 2006
- Peace: A Compilation of Short Teachings, 2009
- Why I Make Myself Unhappy, 2005

DVDs

- Do I Suffer from A.E?
- Nothing Changes & The Enemy Within
- Sayonara to Depression
- Snakes, Roosters and Pigs
- While I Still Can

For more information on these and other books and DVDs, please visit **www.kechara.com/kmp**

All books and DVDs can be purchased online at **www.kechara.com/eshop**

H.E. Tsem Tulku Rinpoche's teachings can also be viewed online on YouTube.com. Search "tsemtulku".

THE PHOTOGRAPHERS

H.E. Tsem Tulku Rinpoche's Liaisons

Some of His Eminence's liaisons (personal assistants) and personal attendants have also contributed their personal photographs to this book. These photographs are especially treasured because many of them were taken during their travels with His Eminence to sacred sites around the world. The liaisons hope that the photographs they have contributed will inspire many readers towards a joyous, peaceful, uplifting journey of spirituality and self-discovery.

Fang Chyi, Chang is an art director by day and performer by night. Fang has worked in many world-class productions and she was nominated for the 'Best Solo Performance (Vocal)' category in the BOH Cameronian Arts Awards, 2006. In May 2008, Fang Chyi was nominated for 'Best Set Design' for her work in *OKIKU: A Tragedy Untold* and she is currently one of Kakiseni Cameronian Arts Award judges. As an extension of her creative soul, she enjoys photography whenever the opportunity arises.

Mun Lee is a multi-talented graphic designer, photographer and dancer, who employs a unique and distinctive angle in capturing the fleeting moments in life. She deconstructs aestheticism as a source of inspiration, resulting in highly original and attractive works. Mun can be contacted on **ms_munlee@yahoo.com**

Wei Yein, Leong says that having the memory of a goldfish forces her to frame moments in her life through the corners of a lens. As a creative writer and an avid traveller, photography has in its own subtle way, taught her how to simplify her life, cut out the clutter, be mindful of the world, and watch out for the little things in life she often takes for granted.

Marcus Lim is an ophthalmologist in Singapore. When not performing surgery, Marcus enjoys taking nature photographs on land and underwater. His photographs have been featured in local and international exhibitions, and have appeared in books and magazines. One of his photographs won Marcus an award in the European Nature Photographer of the Year Competition in 2008. In his next life, Marcus would like to be a professional nature photographer.

Michaelangelo Francisco Moran was born and raised in Jakarta, Indonesia, but has moved to San Francisco to try to become an inspiring artist in the world of new media. He believes there is still much for him to learn and as life is full of obstacles, he is dedicated to confronting these on his journey to becoming a successful designer. He hopes that the designs he creates will leave a lasting impression. His work and portfolio can be viewed on **www.michaelangelomoran.com**

U-En, Ng is a former journalist. As a means of supplementing his income, he sometimes writes plays and occasionally acts in them. He has not been very successful at either of these, nor unfortunately has he been bad enough for people to pay him to do neither. He is, however, very good at doing nothing at all, which is why he is single, lives alone, and has approximately eight friends.

Linda See is an award-winning videographer, with deep interests in film, music, drawing and photography. Her video was selected for the Singapore submission for the World One Minutes exhibition in the Today Art Museum, Beijing, which was part of the cultural programme around the Olympic Games in June 2008. Having lived for two years in Europe, Linda takes every opportunity to combine her passion for photography and art with travel.

Venkat Srinivasan is a writer and photographer based in the United States. He specialises in writing on and around the sciences, and his work has appeared in Wired, GlobalPost, Telegraph and Tehelka, amongst others. He also trained in materials engineering and is a staff engineer at SLAC National Accelerator Labs. His photographs can be seen at **www.flickr.com/photos/doodlematix**

Ben Tan is a Malaysian actor. He studied Fine Arts and Drama at university and later did his Masters in Design Research in London. After working as a Creative Director in Advertising for more than twenty years, Ben has returned to the Theatre and has recently branched out into Film, locally and internationally. Ben has also dabbled in Production Design and is the recipient of the Malaysian National Arts Award for Theatre Design 2009.

Boon Peen, Tee is a self-confessed geek who loves all things high tech. However, she goes back to basics when it comes to photography, shooting predominantly with film using the most basic cameras to capture everyday life. Boon Peen credits her photography club advisor for introducing the world of manual film photography to her when she was 14. Currently based in Singapore, she hopes that her passion for photography will one day allow her to travel in order to experience and capture more.

Felix Tee is a self-made entrepreneur and businessman of international high standing. A co-founder of Unisem Bhd. and the creative force behind a number of smaller businesses, Tee has 17 years of experience in construction, mechanical engineering and high-tech business. He has integrated his interest in technology and passion for nature and transformed it into Casabrina, a unique eco-friendly community development amidst the magical mountains of Pahang. He particularly enjoys photography of nature's scenes surrounding Casabrina **(http://casabrina.net)**.

Gary Yap is a graphic designer and amateur photographer. The image (on page 104) is from his second trip to Rajasthan, India. He admires the civilising influence and cultural assimilation brought about by early Islam so his travels tend towards those countries that have felt the breath of the desert winds blowing out of the Arabian peninsula.

Kien Kiong, Yeo is currently working on a hand-drawn animation feature film, having spent most of his time pondering upon the ever-changing world as a grand kaleidoscope. Photography is one of his favourite past times. In these pictures, he hopes to convey the beauty and harshness of life and death, and intends every photograph to speak a multitude of messages such as struggle, devastation, greed, poverty, love, passion, calmness and happiness.

ACKNOWLEDGEMENTS

The editors of this book wish to thank our kindest Lama, H.E. Tsem Tulku Rinpoche, who has given us thousands of teachings from which these incredible quotations have been extracted. We only wish there were more pages so we could fit them all in!

This beautiful book you are holding would not have been possible without the amazing photographs, which were so kindly contributed by our panel of esteemed photographers. Thank you for sharing your works of art with us which we are sure will bring much inspiration to others.

We are also deeply indebted to many other people who have contributed to the success of this great volume. We extend our warmest thanks to Joan Foo Mahony for her editorial advice, Shirley Maya Tan for her kind and precious contribution, Fang Chyi Chang for her extra efforts, Precious Old China Cafe, J.S. Wong and Kenzo de Tuan, and the whole supportive team at Kechara.

KECHARA

Established in 2000, Kechara is a non-profit Buddhist organisation under the spiritual guidance of His Eminence Tsem Tulku Rinpoche. It is an affiliate of the illustrious 600-year-old Gaden Shartse Monastery, which is now situated in Mundgod, south India. Gaden Shartse Monastery belongs to the holy Gaden Monastery which now houses more than 3,000 monks and is one of the most elite monastic universities in the world.

The Kechara organisation seeks to bring the beautiful, ancient wisdom of Buddhism to as many people as possible around the world. It offers a range of programmes that include introductory classes on Buddhism, prayer sessions and wonderful opportunities to volunteer in Buddhist-related arts, publishing and community service.

While based in Malaysia and Nepal, Kechara also has supporters and friends from all around the world who follow its activities via its website and active, online, social network.

Since its inception, Kechara has grown into several departments:
Kechara House – the main centre, which holds daily prayer sessions, education programmes and diverse Dharma activities.

Kechara Discovery – a travel consultancy which organises pilgrimages to holy places and sources for statues to complement the selection at the outlets.

Kechara InMotion – a film production house.

Kechara Lounge – an information centre and lounge in Boudha Stupa, Kathmandu, Nepal.

Kechara Media & Publications – the publishing arm.

Kechara Paradise – retail outlets in prominent areas of Kuala Lumpur and Penang, offering handicrafts and artifacts from the Himalayan region.

Kechara Oasis – a new-age vegetarian restaurant.

Kechara Saraswati Arts – the first Himalayan arts studio in Southeast Asia.

Kechara Soup Kitchen – a community action group which distributes food to the homeless and urban poor in the Klang Valley, Malaysia.

Kechara Southern Jewel Chapel – a Setrap chapel in Johor Bahru, a city in south Malaysia.

Tsem Kachö Ling – the future spiritual sanctuary and Buddhist learning centre.

If you would like to know more about Kechara, please contact us at:
Kechara House
21-23, Jalan PJU 1/3G,
SunwayMas Commercial Centre,
47301 Petaling Jaya
Selangor, Malaysia

Tel: (+603) 7803 3908
Fax: (+603) 7803 3108

E-mail: care@kechara.com
Website: www.kechara.com

KECHARA MEDIA & PUBLICATIONS

Kechara Media & Publications (KMP) is the publishing arm of the Kechara Buddhist organisation. First established in 2005 by a group of young and dedicated students, KMP's vision is to bring H.E. Tsem Tulku Rinpoche's teachings and the ancient wisdom of Dharma into the context of contemporary living.

KMP, with its committed core team, is continuously researching the latest technologies and other platforms of new media to make our products universally accessible. This includes an upcoming range of e-books, as well as e-learning and multi-media downloads in both English and Chinese.

For more information about KMP, please contact us at:
Kechara Media & Publications Sdn. Bhd.
5-2, Jalan PJU 1/3G,
SunwayMas Commercial Centre,
47301 Petaling Jaya,
Selangor, Malaysia

Tel: (+603) 7805 5691
Fax: (+603) 7805 5690